I0480267

Requests for permission may be made to:

Moni Brodie – Moni@MoniBCosmetics.com

919-885-0695

Cover Photography: Damien Prout/ Crush Photography Studios

Cover Jewelry: Rachel Stewart Jewelry

Table of Contents

ACKNOWLEDGEMENTS

Where would I be without Chill Will & Barb-Ann....My Superman and Wonder Woman. Together they set the stage and became the perfect example of unconditional love. There's not a day that goes by that I don't think of them and miss the sound of their voice, smell of their hair, and bright smiles. Thank you for meeting that fateful night in Philly and beginning a love that lasts today through our memories of you.

My main dude, Bryce. He's simply amazing. I cannot wait to see him become the man I know he's destined to be. His very presence makes me better and knowing he's looking to me as an example of a woman encourages me every day. I say all the time you came at a time when I needed you more than you needed me. You give my life meaning in a way that is unexplainable and there's no better job than being your Mom. You are simply hands down the dopest 12 year old I know. Keep being resilient, brave, and good to people. You won't always get it right and Lord knows I don't either but as long as your heart is good you can make it right. I will love you for the rest of your life and even long after.

To all of my family, friends, and precious inner circle of "Girls" I love you and thank you for all you've poured into me throughout my entire life. I'm forever grateful.

To all of my fellow entrepreneurs, thank you for your inspiration and perseverance. Watching you keeps me going and lets me know if you can do it, there's nothing to stop me from doing the same.

My friend and Brand Strategist Tunisha Brown is absolutely everything! When I needed help with exposure for my own beauty brand she was just getting started with her new venture Impact Brand Strategists but the funny thing is, I trusted her right from the beginning. I knew she would have my best interest at heart and that proved to be the case and more. Thank you for believing in me and partnering with me to create magic.

To my Bearded BAE, your support and hearing you say "I'm so proud of you" has meant so much to me. You get me, you understand my purpose.....thank you.

My inspiration for this workbook came from a desire to want to help. Soon after launching my own beauty brand I was immediately contacted by people asking me how they could do the same. Initially I was hesitant about sharing information simply because I didn't think I'd developed it enough to tell anyone else what they needed to do. I didn't want to hand over bad tips, strategies, or have them chasing down the wrong path. So I waited, and waited, and waited, and then one day I simply said to myself…it's time.

I wholeheartedly believe if you tell people what to do they may get it momentarily, however, if you teach them you then put them in a powerful position. Providing the tools to help others be successful is why I decided to write this workbook. I hope it will be just the starting point to what will be an amazing journey for you and I'm proud of you for taking the first step. Even in fear you have to do it anyway…and look at you, you're doing it!

HOW TO

CREATE YOUR OWN BEAUTY BRAND

INTRODUCTION

"I'm not a businessman, I'm a business...man."
Jay-Z

I've always believed there's no way you can truly be successful with one source of income. From Jay-Z to Oprah and other notables, their status on the Forbes list does not come from just one business or venture. Instead, their wealth is attained by having multiple sources of income. It is with this belief that I started *Moni B. Cosmetics* in an effort to offer products to makeup clients as an add-on to the services I already provided. Keep this in mind at all times...whatever it is you love to do, find more than one way to make money from your love. I promise it won't feel quite like work when you are constantly moving, breathing, and living in your purpose. So if you're a chef you may go the route of teaching cooking classes, offering 1-on-1 instruction, even providing catering services. What about an author, you can write your own books, articles for magazines/blogs, or serve as a ghost writer for others. It's not that hard to think of different ways to profit from your business, but what may cause some hesitation is how to make it all happen. Between lack of time and resources I know it can be hard to figure it all out no matter how bad you want to bring your dreams into reality.

This workbook is designed to give you a **starting** point to help you create your own beauty brand. The thought alone is cool, right? A tube of lipstick, a jar of hair pomade, or a bar of soap with your logo on the box is a huge accomplishment and with these guidelines but what does it take to get there? Again, this book is only the beginning for you which means nothing will happen if you don't do the work. I think it's only right for me to let you know that creating your own beauty brand won't be easy as it's not a turn key business or in other words you can't just pay a fee and flip a switch. Unlike well known brands, you may not have the well skilled team in your corner ready to support your new endeavor. It will take your time, focus, and consistency to be successful, but the good news is that it can be done and I will be with you every step of the way.

If there is any doubt about you creating your own beauty brand because you are comparing what you want to do with all of the household names, let it go. From L'Oréal founded by Eugène Schueller in 1909 to Maybelline started by 19-year old entrepreneur Thomas Lyle Williams in 1915, they all were once small and unknown. Even one of the most popular lines in the world, Make-up Art Cosmetics aka M.A.C. founded in Canada by Frank Toscan and Frank Angelo had small beginnings with just their inner circle but quickly grew and is now one of the top 3 global brands.

Here's what I'm saying, we all have to start somewhere and the more you invest your time and resources into doing it right the first time the better your chances of growing into being a household name will be. I don't know about you but I always want to win and I surely want to see you do the same. Okay, enough of my ranting...

LET'S GET DOWN TO BUSINESS!

MAKIN' MONEY MOVES

Before we jump into the steps and strategies outlined in this workbook, I want to assure you there is in fact money to be made in this industry. According to MarketResearch.com, the cosmetics industry (which is made up of 6 categories including color cosmetics aka makeup and skin care products) was projected to make $62 billion in 2016 just in the United States alone (the number increases when you consider the global market). The steady growth over the past few years is due in part to the introduction of indie labels to the market. With brands such as *ColourPop*, *Kylie Cosmetics*, *Juvia's Place, Camille Rose Naturals, Hairizon, and* so many more making an impact amongst beauty enthusiasts, it's not as hard as one might think to become a part of this billion dollar industry.

Although major brands still hold a large percentage of the market, make no mistake it's the smaller brands – like the one you want to create – that contribute to the overall growing revenue in the cosmetics industry. What does that mean for you? It means you **can** have a piece of the pie! Plain and simple you can do this and you can get paid while doing it.

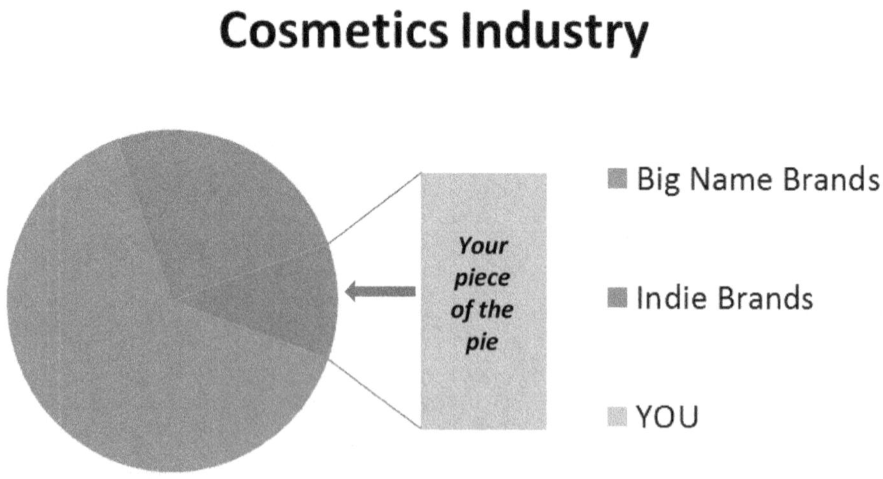

The Function of This Workbook

As each person is different, the path you take to reach your goals will also differ. However, there are always key steps in order to get there. I mean in order to walk you've got to put one foot in front of the other, right? Some may have a sway in their hips and others may be as stiff as a board but the PROCESS is the same for both. The same rings true for you…there are steps almost everyone must take in order to create a successful beauty brand. Please note, this workbook will focus more on the product itself including how to create, distribute and fund your brand but there is a bit more to the business side we will briefly address in Chapter 4.

The function of this workbook is to help you find your own way through the steps that worked for me. Although I am in the makeup industry, this process can work for any beauty brand as the end result is usually the same…to make women look and feel better.

Here are the steps we will discuss as a part of this process:

1. Finding Your Niche
2. Identifying Your Brand
3. Creating Your Product
4. The Business of BEAUTY
5. Where To Offer Your Products
6. The Importance of Social Media
7. How To Fund Your Beauty Brand

"No niche is
too small
if it's yours."
-Seth Godin

1

FINDING YOUR NICHE

Although you will start as a small indie label, the expectation will be for you to compete in terms of quality and price with all of the major brands. I know that may not make sense after all, how can you be expected to compare to an established brand. But the reality is customers won't care that you're just getting started and may need some time to get it together. It is not their problem or concern that you've had to change vendors and adjust ingredients. That's why 'getting it right the first time' is going to be so important. It's okay to tweak things along the way I mean we wake up to a different version of Facebook every other day, but you will need to have a strong foundation from the start.

In order to hit the ground running with your beauty brand you will have to find your lane or your niche. Establishing early on what is different about either your products and/or your story will help set the stage for all that will come after. I often tell people that no matter how original you think your product may be, there's almost nothing new under the sun. Let's take lipstick for example, to the user it will serve the same purpose – to apply color to the lips, therefore, you must identify early on what makes your brand stand out.

As I stated earlier, I knew I wanted to create a brand that included products I could offer to my existing makeup clientele. For me, color cosmetics was the natural choice for a few reasons including my love for makeup. I was definitely one of those little girls that would play in my Mom's lipsticks and even mix colors trying to create my personal style. My Barbie collection rivaled that of Mattel's and each doll had their own beauty regimen.

STEP OUT OF YOUR BOX

Offering lipstick as my first product proved to be a very smart move and allowed me to connect with customers from the beginner to the expert. I had so much fun creating colors I hoped would appeal to everyone and I even stepped outside of my box to ensure my line catered to all women. Prior to launching my first colors, I was not a fan of dark colors or matte lipsticks. I'm not sure why I didn't like darker colors, I think it had to do with MY idea of what was considered beautiful. Any who, follow me for just a few moments.

To help save on cost I enlisted the help of family and friends to serve as 'product testers' and every time I introduced a new color one family member in particular kept asking "Will everything be bright and glossy?" She doesn't know this but I would always get a bit annoyed with her question. I mean, the colors were amazing and consistent with what I wanted to provide as well as what was trending in the makeup world. But after further research, I found that she was right....I didn't offer much outside of what I liked and was comfortable wearing. There may have been a lot of missed money, exposure, and opportunities if I had not simply took a step outside of my box. Not to mention some of the most popular colors and best selling items where those I didn't initially include as a part of the launch collection. So, don't be afraid to do things that are a bit different or take you away from what makes you comfortable, your customers are what is most important and you don't want to be limited. Bottom line, if you don't give your audience what they want they will find it with someone else.

IT'S YOUR TURN

It's time for you to jump on in and tackle your first exercise which may be the most critical. This will help provide clarity and narrow down your "lane". In this first step, we will use the next few pages to either develop or list the products you plan to offer. Make sure to capture **everything** in this section and don't worry about whether or not it will work at this time. As we continue to develop your brand throughout this workbook, you will have the opportunity to revise, remove, and expand on your ideas.

YOUR PRODUCTS

You don't have to look very far when figuring out what products you want to offer, just start with yourself. Think about what you're passionate about and what you'd want as the customer. Here's a little known fact...before settling on makeup for *Moni B. Cosmetics*, I briefly thought about creating a skin care line. My thought process was that if your skin doesn't look good no amount of makeup will help. While this is most certainly a true statement, after discussions with trusted friends and long time clients I realized makeup made my eyes dance. It will be your love for the products that will ultimately make the difference to your customers and they will see it when you speak about your beauty brand.

Lastly, don't be afraid to be different! Now is not that time to be fearful and shy but rather allow all of your ideas to come together and create something magical. You've been dreaming about doing this for quite some time and I always say, SCARED MONEY MAKES NO MONEY! If what you want to offer as a part of your line is something you've never seen before go for it as it can possibly allow you to start off with a product that immediately draws attention. If it doesn't work that's okay too because success is not in your failures but in what you learn from them.

List the products you'd like to offer

**Tip – Think about which products you'd like to offer when you launch your line, what products you want to offer down the road, and any future products and ideas you have once you've built a customer base. You will have a chance to organize your products based on this criteria during this chapter.*

Products Cont'd

List the products you'd like to offer

**Tip – Make sure your products flow and customers can easily connect them back to your brand. As you grow, you will be able to branch off into other directions once you have a dedicated base.*

NEEDS AND DEMANDS

Now that you've established the products you will offer, it's time to associate the need or demand each one will fill for your customers. Simply having a product you think is cool, pretty, or nice is not enough. There are two things you must keep in mind during this exercise:

a)Who will your brand help

b)Who will find value in what you have to offer

Will your line cater to those with sensitive skin or vegans? Do you have a quick skin care process that will help save time for busy Moms? Use the section on the next page to do the following:

1)List your product

2)Indicate the need and/or demand

a) If this list includes products that need to be used together, make sure to list them consecutively

In addition to the need and demand your product will fill, we will also use this section to highlight any special ingredients or processes. Including all natural or high end ingredients will help your brand stand out from the rest. It will also give you a level of uniqueness that can possibly help you make more sales. We will speak more about Handmade vs. Mass Produced products so if this does not necessarily apply to you at this time, you can always come back to this section.

**Tip – If this exercise is hard to do at first, go back to your list of products and think about WHY you want to include them. Even if the answer is simply you think it will make a lot of money include that statement. We will come back to this section a bit later.*

What need or demand are you filling with your product(s)?

Product Name	Explain Need or Demand
Ex: Eyeshadow	*Formulated for wearers with sensitive skin*

Do your products include special ingredients or formulations that will make it stand out from others? Instead of regular milk you may use goat milk or instead of processed oils you prefer to use refined.

Product Name	Special Ingredients or processes
Face Wash	*Aloe vera gel, essential oils*

WHO ARE YOU?

Now that you're clear on what's to be included in your line, let's focus on your story or your WHY. Behind every brand is a reason why it exists. One of the hair care lines I've seen all over social media these days is *E'TAE Naturals* and per the feedback from customers it's an amazing product. I find myself stopping to watch their video testimonials each time it comes up in my feed and getting super excited to see how silky and shiny the hair turns out to be at the end. While it is loved by users all over the world, its founder Kisha Tompkins-Hudson was inspired to develop the line to care for her daughter's hair.

Defining your why helps to connect customers to the heart of your brand and give it a personal voice and personality. Your reason should not come off as self-serving so put some time into this exercise. The end goal should always point back to how your beauty brand can help someone else. This exercise will help prepare you for Chapter 2 as we dig a bit deeper into this topic.

What is YOUR story? Identify your WHY.

THINGS TO THINK ABOUT

- Stay on top of trends in your particular industry. How do your products tie into what's current?

- Do you know which product in your specific industry are the hottest based on customer use? Ex. Gel nail polish vs. regular nail polish.
  - Take some time to conduct your own research by asking family, friends, as well as calling and/or visiting local establishments offering services geared towards your products.

- Pay attention to any ingredients recently reported or known in the past to have been harmful or dangerous.
  - Consider removing the product or find an alternate if handmade
  - If mass produced, discuss options with your vendor.

- Although you will create your own lane, stay away from items that will make you seem like a copycat. I know a lipstick is a lipstick but try your best to always make certain there is a differentiation where you can. i.e. Color, Packaging, and/or Product Names

FINDING YOUR NICHE NOTES

FINDING YOUR NICHE NOTES

"Branding is
the art
of becoming knowable,
likeable,
and trustable."
-John Jantsch

2

IDENTIFYING YOUR BRAND

Now that you've figured out your niche, it's time to work on branding what you've created. Branding pretty much means defining how customers will see you in the market place or how you establish an identity for your business. Who you are needs to be very clear as mixed messages cause confusion and ultimately a lack of trust.

One area of confusion when it comes to this subject is the difference between BRANDING vs. MARKETING. Here's the major difference, ***Branding*** as stated above is how your brand will be seen while ***Marketing*** is making sure that it is in a place in front of the right people to be seen. Does that make sense? It's the difference between having a cute outfit to wear so you can meet a new guy and being in a room or event where that new guy will see you. This workbook places more emphasis on developing and creating your beauty brand as you need to have something top notice in place before you invest too much of your resources in marketing. However, the two most certainly go hand in hand and once you have created a solid product the next step will be to create a marketing plan to gain exposure. Trust me, it can be very frustrating to go through the process outlined in this workbook only to fail in the area of effective marketing.

Let's first come up with a name for your beauty brand. You may wonder why we didn't do this in the very beginning and here's why...I wanted you to build your entire business on your products. Sometimes we get so caught up in coming up with a cute or catchy name that we lose sight of what really matters. Having a catchy name won't mean a thing if what you have to offer is of poor quality. You may attract business at first, but it certainly won't keep the dollars rolling in. Don't get me wrong I'm not saying that what you call your business or an amazing logo isn't important, however, it's like building a palace with beautiful fixtures on sand. It may look pretty from the outside but due to the weak foundation, it will eventually fall.

ALL IN A NAME

I was working with a young lady to develop her beauty business not long ago and we started chatting about the name. She was more excited about what she wanted to call her brand than anything else but once we started to dive into the process outlined in this workbook, she seemed to become less enthusiastic. Now I'm all about sensing someone's negative energy and working to change the direction so we stopped to address the issue. To make a long story short, her name while great didn't really match what she was working to build.

It will be important when choosing a name to make sure it flows with what you are creating and doesn't leave customers confused. The last thing you want is for them to spend too much time wondering what you do or thinking too hard to figure out what products you offer. Although people may not have known who Moni B. was, putting the word "cosmetics" at the end helped them to immediately have an idea of what I sold as a part of my brand. We will use the next section to come up with your name.

List your ideas here for the name of your business and why that name appeals to you.

Beauty Brand Name	Why?

**Tip - Come up with more than one and poll family, friends, or trusted business associates to see which one sticks. Also do a search to see if there are others with the same name. You don't want to deal with copyright issues and/or brand confusion from names that are too similar.*

KNOWING YOUR COMPETITION

To further identify who you are, you need to know who and what is already out there that has a similar business and/or product. I'm sure you've seen memes that tell you things like "don't worry about your competition" or "only focus on your lane if you want to reach the top" and while part of that is true, how can you know if you are the best or need to make improvements if you are oblivious to what your customers see.

Now, here's where things can get a little squirrely, some may agree and some won't but my goal was always to set my goals high. What I learned is that your average customer either does not know or won't care that you don't have the staff and money behind you like the big names. All they know is what they like and will measure your product based on how it compares to their favorite. With that being said, keep in mind...**YOUR COMPETITION IS NOT THE LADY DOWN THE STREET OR SOMEONE LOCAL THAT HAS A SIMILAR PRODUCT.** So what Sally has a line of nail polish too, as I stated before customers will not compare you to Sally. They will instead hold you to the same quality as OPI or Essie. I'm not at all saying you shouldn't be aware of local competition or other indie labels but what I am saying is that you should always think like your customer and set your goals high.

List your competition and what you think makes them a competitor.

Competitor	Why?

Cont'd
List your competition and what you think makes them a competitor.

Competitor	Why?

**Tip - RESEARCH, RESEARCH, RESEARCH. Start out with those names you've heard of then use your resources (Internet, family, and friends) to list others. You want at least 7-10 companies on this list.*

The purpose of this list is so you know what customers prefer. It's not to copy their products or style but to be successful, you need to know who your future customers see as their favorite brands.

YOUR IDEAL CUSTOMER

In the last chapter we spoke about your Why or the reason you created your beauty brand. Let's now turn the focus on your WHO or the person that will most likely purchase from you. The only way to make certain your product ends up in the right hands is to know exactly who they are. Will men or women be your primary customer? Do you anticipate millennials or baby boomers as your primary base? All of these questions will help you to understand how to create products and build your brand around an audience who want what you have to offer.

When I first created *Moni B. Cosmetics* I knew I had to know exactly who would be purchasing my products as honestly what I was offering was not unique or one of a kind. Far from rocket science I had lipstick and lip gloss and while I knew I offered quality products, it would take combining that quality with knowing the WHO that would make the difference. One of the first things I did was to think about who I already attracted to my services as a makeup artist. What I noticed was that most of my clients were makeup newbies as word spread about the way in which I explained each step of the process. I was also known for being patient and providing 1-on-1 lessons that were both fun and informative. It was at that very moment I decided my ideal customer would be someone that was either new to makeup or didn't know very much about how to apply or pick the best colors.

To be honest, your ideal customer will reveal themselves to you after some time so if this exercise isn't very easy for you to do at first that's perfectly fine. Also, having a specific person your brand speaks to does not mean that others won't support you. Think about athletic shoes, in particular sneakers...their ideal customer is usually one that actively plays sports or has a dedicated work out regimen but I know lots of people that are sedentary and wear sneakers on a regular basis. So knowing who your brand will speak to be is not about inclusion but more about sending the right message to the right people.

Think about your ideal customer. What does he/she look like and how will he/she feel about your brand. Can you see it? Describe him/her below:

____

____

____

____

____

____

____

____

____

____

____

____

**Tip – Include their age, race, how they wear their hair, what kind of food they like to eat, etc. In other words, be VERY specific. Will this be the only person that will buy your products…of course not, but in order to make your products speak to your ideal customer*

A POPPIN' LOGO

Having a recognizable logo is key in creating a voice for your brand in the market place. It's normal to want to have something colorful and pretty but, most of our favorite brands have logos that are **S**imple and **C**lean. Also think about reproducing your logos for labels, paraphernalia, and in print. A logo that is too busy or has lots of colors can start to get mangled over time. I know you want a dope logo but my advice **KEEP IT SIMPLE**. You can always add some graphics for specific products, but start off with something that isn't too much.

Below I've highlighted some recognizable brands and their logos. Do you have an existing logo? Is it clean and easy for customers to spot in the sea of all of the others on the shelves? How many colors do you have? Does it tie into your overall brand?

**Logos used for illustration purposes*

LABELS 101

Once you've decided on a logo there are many options to label your products.

-*Hot Stamping* – Uses pre-dried ink at hot temperatures and is placed on your items. It's very permanent and costs can vary but it is the most expensive of your options. It lasts longer than the other methods

-*Silk Screen* – This option offers the ability to add textures to your bottles or tubes.

-*Offset Printing*– Uses printing plates

-*Self Stick* – Usually the least expensive and quickest turn around. It is where the logo is printed on labels and manually placed on products. Many types of paper can be used to mimic hot stamp and ink print results. With this option, you have more control over logo/label placement. You can use a professional printing company or print yourself.

The method you use is a personal decision, however, make sure it's professional looking and easy to read. Also, if your product requires it make sure to include the size of your bottle or tube and the ingredients.

Use this page to sketch your logo and if that's not your forte, describe your logo so if you need to outsource this part of creating your brand you know exactly what you want.

**Tip – Remember to keep in mind...Clean & Simple.*

IDENTIFYING YOUR BRAND NOTES

IDENTIFYING YOUR BRAND NOTES

"The secret
to building
great products
is not creating
awesome features,
it's to
make your
users awesome."
-Kathy Sierra

3

CREATING YOUR PRODUCTS

It's time to pinpoint exactly how you will create your products. Now my assumption up to this point is that you have a beauty brand that's in your head and you're working to develop it or that you have an existing brand that needs some help. The reason I mention this is because you should have some idea of how to create the product you want to offer and how you want it to look. But here's the most important part, **make certain you create products and packaging that keep the customer in mind.** Maybe it's cheaper to do a spray nozzle over a pump or it may be easier to find white tubes instead of black...but always keep what your ideal customer will want as what is most important. I mean honestly if they don't like that nozzle or it's hard to open...they won't buy your shampoo or face cream. In this section we will focus on things to keep in mind whether your products are handmade or mass produced.

Handmade

We will start with products that will be made by hand or produced directly by you. Here is what you need to consider:

•What are your ingredients?
•Has your product been tested to ensure it does not cause any skin irritations or other issues (keep in mind there are always exceptions no matter how much testing you may do)

- Depending on the product you can have friends and family serve as testers.
- If it's more involved you may want to enlist the help of a chemist.

•What sources will you use to buy your ingredients in bulk?
•Where will you get your packaging?

- What's the best way to package your products so there are no spills or leaks especially when it's time to ship.

•What type of labels will work best

STORAGE

As you begin to fulfill orders, you will need to ensure you have them ready to distribute as quickly as possible. The only way to do this is to prepare them ahead of time so storage is a key component. There may be some products that will need to be filled as ordered but as much as you can have ready for immediate orders, the better for you.

Many times handmade products include sensitive and/or natural ingredients that may become otherwise unusable in certain conditions. Options may be an additional refrigerator in your home or even renting a storage facility conducive to cooler temperatures. In addition, the shelf life of your products can vary for handmade products. Be certain to include expiration dates and instructions for customers to get the longest use for their products. For instance, if your foot scrub can only last up to a year based on research by your own use or your designated testers, place this information on your labels.

Handmade

To determine which suppliers to use there's only one option, research and create a list including location, price, and products offered. Keep in mind, you may need to get your supplies from more than one company and that's perfectly fine. Use the next 2 pages to create your list. This list should include sources for both PACKAGING and the INGREDIENTS USED TO MAKE THE PRODUCT. To do this research make sure you visit websites, search online reviews, call, ask questions, get samples, and start to build relationships with those you're most interested in to see which one will suit your needs. As previously stated, your customer's needs and making them feel amazing when using your products is your top priority. You want do what's cost effective without risking quality.

Where are you getting your supplies?

Supplier name	Contact Info	Products offered	Cost (Unit of Mea.)
John Doe & Friends	*123 Wisconsin Drive Bronx, NY 10452 718-555-1234 john@friends.com*	*Boxes, tubes, shea butter, filling trays*	*$.14 per tube (Black) $. 25 shea butter*

Handmade

Where are you getting your supplies (cont'd)?

Supplier name	Contact Info	Products offered	Cost (Unit of Mea.)

List your top 5 suppliers, why?

Mass produced

Let me say here that whether your products are handmade or mass produced, what matters most is the quality. That's it.....QUALITY! I want to drive that point home as much as possible during this process as it will make or break your brand. Everything else may look and sound great but your product should be the **star of the show**.

Here is what you should consider if your products are mass produced:

- What sources will you use to buy your products in bulk?
- What are the ingredients?
- Will you buy private label or create your own products with a chemist?
- Where will you get your packaging (you won't have this issue with private label companies.
- If using private label, are there an adequate number of options
- What type of labeling will work best
- What storage option would be best (see pg. 32)

PRIVATE LABEL

There was once a time when it took both a lot of time and resources to start your own beauty brand, however, with the introduction of Private Label companies it's much easier and cost effective. Private label companies are simply those that manufacture products which allow you to place your own label on products that have already been created. You simply place your logo using the label option that works best (many offer label options as well) and you can more easily launch your brand. However, please keep in mind that the product alone will not make you successful so you will still need to follow the steps outlined in this workbook. There are quite a few private label companies you can find during your research.

This option is also popular as it allows you to buy products as you need them as opposed to buying in bulk. The exception would be Private Label brands from China as although they offer the cheapest per product cost, the MOQ (*Minimum Order Quantity*) usually starts at 10,000 units. Now if you think you can sell that much out the gate then it is your best option if you go the private label route but if not, ordering from local companies would be best. Lastly, using Private Label companies can also allow you to skip the step of testing as they have already conducted the research. Most also offer additional services to ensure your product is one of a kind and exclusive to you.

> **Tip – Many private label companies can also work with you to produce your own products as opposed to choosing from their catalog. Another option most offer is filling tubes you create or purchase yourself. Make sure you explore all of their services and ask questions to help you make an informed decision.*

Mass produced

Use this section to list companies you can purchase products already created (Private Label) or those you can work with to create your own.

Use the section below to list potential partners

Company name	Contact Info	Products offered	Cost (Unit of Mea.)

**Tip – Not sure where to start, simply conduct a search for 'Private Label' online and several companies will display.*

CREATING YOUR PRODUCTS NOTES

CREATING YOUR PRODUCTS NOTES

"If people like you
they'll listen to
you but if
they trust you
they'll do
business
with you."
-Zig Ziglar

4

THE BUSINESS OF BEAUTY

Up until now we've focused on the creative side of creating your brand because that's where you should focus your time and attention for the purposes of this workbook. However, as with all things in which money is concerned... BEAUTY IS A BUSINESS and you should never forget that. Another element of your business that will make or break it is the actual business model you put together to ensure you are successful.

You should absolutely have a business plan in place and execute that plan at every level of your beauty brand. Don't skip this step because "you know, it's just makeup or face wash", etc. While money shouldn't be your driving force (it should be to help people and fill a need) you will have to make your 'coins' are coming in so you can grow. While I won't delve too deep into this chapter, it is time in the process to do the following:

DEVELOP YOUR BUSINESS PLAN

A Business plan is a blueprint that includes the strategies and objectives for your business. It gives you a roadmap to follow and helps you stay on target to reach your goals. Your business plan should have several pieces to cover every aspect of your business including financial and marketing.

RETAIL COST VS. PRODUCTION COST

In order to know if you've made a profit, you have to know the cost to produce or purchase your product vs. the retail cost or the price you charge your customers. I'm always asked, "Moni, how much should I charge?" and honestly that's a loaded question as it really is dependent upon how much it cost to create the product. You are the person who will determine the retail cost and one of the ways to keep retail cost down is to keep production cost down. That's why *Chapter 3* where we discuss *Creating Your Products* is so important specifically researching suppliers. Use your business plan to figure out your overall financial goal and price you products so they gain you maximum profit while being competitive.

THE IMPORTANCE OF A MENTOR

As you develop your business you will face challenges that may best be explained and understood by someone that has already walked the path you are attempting to travel. Having a mentor you can consult and seek for guidance is vital to your growth. Please note this person does NOT have to be in the beauty business to serve as a mentor. You should be seeking someone with business knowledge and experience and that can be found in any industry.

ADDITIONAL AREAS OF BUSINESS

•Determine Business organization (Sole proprietorship, LLC, etc.)
•Open business bank account (includes PayPal or Square Up Account to easily accept online and credit card payments)
•Determine tax rate for your city/state/country (you will need this for your website or store front)
•There are additional costs highlighted in *Chapter 7* – How To Fund Your Beauty Brand

Let's move on to an aspect of your business you will need to have in place at its inception, let's talk...**CUSTOMER SERVICE**. This can get lost especially with new businesses and I'll tell you right now, it's an unspoken good or evil. As with any business how your customers perceive how you handle them will be the determining factor as to whether or not they will return. The old adage "The customer is always right " applies to your beauty brand just like any other business.

Building a relationship with your customers is key so make sure you take the time to create amazing customer service. With beauty brands it will mean including this part of your business model in great depth when building your business plan as products cannot be recycled (ex. once a lipstick is used by one customer it's unsanitary of course to use it as a tester or resell).

I will use the next two sections to provide some potential scenarios and allow you to describe how you would handle them in the space provided. Remember, this is a part of the business side that you must learn how to properly deal with in order to create a brand customers trust.

Susan purchased a body butter that her friend loved but she hates. She contacts you to return. What do you do?

____

____

____

____

____

____

**Tip – Always think about how you'd want to be treated if you were the customer. Your motto should always be "Make It Right". There will be exceptions but generally speaking, do all you can to maintain the customer and preserve the relationship. Nothing travels faster than a bad experience.*

Danielle received her order in the mail but the lipstick color should've been red but it's pink. She's a bit angry, what do you do?

Kim likes the hair serum she received but she's not quite sure how to make it work for her hair. She contacts you for some guidance and suggestions. What do you tell her?

THE BUSINESS OF BEAUTY NOTES

THE BUSINESS OF BEAUTY NOTES

"Sell
yourself
first if
you
want to
sell
anything."
-Burt Lancaster

5

WHERE TO OFFER YOUR PRODUCTS

Something you must keep in mind when you begin selling your products is that people need to understand and connect with YOU. I know we've already spoken about how to ***Identify Your Brand*** (Chapter 3) but, I think it's important to mention it once again.

You can't offer a product that you've never tried and expect for your sales to be through the roof. It just doesn't happen that way. You have to learn how to sell YOU or at least make certain that your brand has your voice both online via your social media platforms and in person otherwise, you won't make money. One of the reasons I believe I have done great with *Moni B. Cosmetics* is because I allowed people to get to know me. When customers buy products from my business many of them feel like they are buying from a friend although they've never met me. This relationship will then spill over to every aspect of your business so when you announce sales, events, and new products they'll be ready to see what you have to offer. Keep in mind this may take some time to build but it is vital to establish this from the start. Remember people want you to be **real and authentic**. Having a clear understanding of who you are will ensure that wherever you decide to sell your products, customers will come to you.

CREATING YOUR WEBSITE

One of the easiest and most effective ways to distribute/offer your products is through your own website. While it can be fairly easy to create, I would suggest hiring a professional for this step in the process if you are not equipped and knowledgeable to do so yourself. Here's the main reason why you should not take on this task, **an ineffective website will make you lose money**! It's not simply enough for people to be able to access your products and services online but you have to also make it easy for potential customers to view, purchase, and exit without a hitch. Whereas it may cost a few hundred dollars to invest in a quality site, the rewards will be much greater If hiring a professional is not in your budget at this time, there are temporary options to help such as Big Cartel and SquareSpace that provide templates and can link with PayPal or offer other payment options. These templates can literally have your website (aka online store) up and running in a matter of minutes. However, please note there are limitations to the functionality of these options so you should still plan to include a professional in your budget as soon as possible.

Much like your social media presence (*Chapter 6*), your website serves as a voice for your brand. Customers that may never see or meet you will be drawn to your products through what they see online. See the steps below to creating your website whether you do it yourself or hire a professional:

- Purchase domain name (it's best to simply use your company name)
- Research sites offering similar products to give you an idea of how you want your website designed (you will want to do this step regardless of who sets up your website. Either you can pick a template with a similar layout or you have somewhere to start when discussing with your website designer)
- Hire a Professional or sign up for one of the recommended eCommerce sites above
- During this time you should make certain you have quality pictures, product descriptions, price, your brand story (*Chapter 1 – Your Why)* and clear instructions to add to your website
- Even after your website has launched, you will have an opportunity to add or make changes to it

There will be other pieces you may want to add but this is a starting point and will help you in the beginning stages. As you begin to sell your products you will determine additional website needs.

**Tip – Also consider Fiverr to hire a professional to develop your website or even barter your products with the services of a professional to cut costs.*

In addition to your own website, there are additional online outlets to offer your beauty brand and reach new customers. Did you know that you can sell your products right from your Facebook Business Page? That's right you can set up your Facebook business page like an online store so customers don't have to stop scrolling their timeline to check you out. It's super easy to set up and is another way to engage your audience.

If your products are handmade, consider Etsy in addition to your own website and/or Facebook. What are some other online communities where you can offer your products?

Tip – Think about partnering with complimentary businesses and having a pop-up shop (you literally pop-up and create a storefront experience for your customer.). This can be done at an actual storefront for a business or in places such as art galleries, hotel suites, or community centers. No matter the location, you want to provide the same level of service you would if you had a store.

This chapter has focused more on alternate places to sell beauty brands because the majority of you will not want to immediately open a store. As I've stated, creating your own beauty brand is not a turn key business and takes some time to build so putting your resources into a full store out the gate may be a bit premature and costly. However, if having a store is something you want to do from the start or down the road there are costs associated you must take into account. See below for a brief overview of the types of expenses you will incur.

The actual cost associated with each expense will vary based on the size of the store, city/state/country, and of course your specific store location (mall vs. stand alone) costs for example.

Expense	Notes
Location	Rent or Lease
Staff	Salary and/or commission based
Utilities	Based on where the story is located this could be included or not
Store Signage	Window displays, instore signage
Products	You will usually need more product for an actual store
Marketing	In addition to social media, advertising in local publications will help drive traffic to your location
Additional costs	Maintenance, extra staff during holidays, cash register, building insurance

**Tip – There are stores that offer co-op programs where your products can be sold for a percentage of sales or minimal rent. Consider monthly events like home parties or 'look & see' parties so people can try your products first hand. Lastly, including your products in 'swag bags' or as giveaways is a great cost-effective way to get exposure for your brand. Use social media to find happenings in your local or surrounding area.*

WHERE TO OFFER YOUR PRODUCTS NOTES

WHERE TO OFFER YOUR PRODUCTS NOTES

"We don't have
a choice
on whether
we do social
media,
the question is
how well we do it."
-Erik Qualman

6

THE IMPORTANCE OF SOCIAL MEDIA

There's no question as to whether or not you should be on social media. It's absolutely necessary and without it you will miss out on customers, money, and opportunities. It's been proven that whenever someone hears of a new brand, product, or company the first thing they do is search for them on social media. Without a social media presence you pretty much don't exist to potential customers. With 2.46 billion global users per Statista, one of the leading statistics companies on the internet, think about the potential of building a solid voice online.

It's amazing to be able to reach people in countries you may never get to travel with a simple click of your thumb. The first time I had a user contact me from England and then Paris, I was convinced of the power of social media. The most important part about building your social media presence is engaging your audience as often as possible. But please don't do this by constantly selling your products and sharing links to your website. Instead, develop a relationship with your followers through posts on a daily basis with information mixed with things to make them laugh, smile, and feel good. No one ever wants to feel like all you do is sell, sell, sell.

As you may not be sure where your customers are on social media early on, the best thing to do is use them all. Each platform captures a different audience so although you will focus most on the platform your ideal customer is likely to use (Chapter 2), don't alienate the other platforms. Okay, from Chapter 2 - who is your ideal customer. By now you may have added on a few characteristics.

Who is your ideal customer?

What are some similarities between you and your ideal customer? (This will help when you create posts)

**Tip – Don't have the time to post on social media sites, look into hiring a Social Media Manager dedicated to building your audience.*

Now let's figure out which social media platform your ideal customer will use most, think about what she/he wants to see on a daily basis. It's okay to try a few different posts at different times of the day to determine which one gets the most engagement. The most popular social media platforms are listed below along with age and gender demographics to give you an idea of where your customer may access your posts. However when posting remember, IT'S ALWAYS ABOUT WHAT YOUR CUSTOMER WANTS TO SEE vs. WHAT YOU WANT TO SHARE. You want to be seen as a resource so that your potential customers come looking for you. Become an authority in your industry through your social media presence and I guarantee you will receive support simply because you will be seen as an expert.

Look at it this way, social media is like a bridge to building a solid relationship with people that don't know you and you may never meet. Each post lays the foundation for a stronger bridge that will lead to more follows, likes, and views. The stronger your bridge the more opportunity to sell your products. While each platform has strategies built in to help businesses advertise and gain exposure, for the purposes of this workbook we will focus on selecting which of the popular sites your ideal customer will use.

FACEBOOK
75% Men; 83% Women
Age: 18-29 **(88%)**, 30-49 **(64%)**, 50-64 **(72%)**, 65+ **(62%)**

INSTAGRAM
26% Men; 38% Women
Age: 18-29 **(59%)**, 30-49 **(33%)**, 50-64 **(33%)**, 65+ **(8%)**

TWITTER
24% Men; 25% Women
Age: 18-29 **(36%)**, 30-49 **(23%)**, 50-64 **(21%)**, 65+ **(10%)**

SNAPCHAT
24% Men; 23% Women
Age: 18-29 **(56%)**, 30-49 **(13%)**, 50+**(9%)**

**Source: The collected data comes from the Pew Social Media Update 2016 report as well as the self-reported information from over 1 billion Facebook profiles of users over the age of 18 pulled from the Facebook Audience Insights Tool.*

Still not sure what you should post. Here are some examples from both my Instagram and Facebook accounts. As you can see, they are lighthearted and do not necessarily sell my products but instead are targeted to offer information and/or make my audience feel good.

**Tip – All of these posts were made using an app called Canva. Canva provides templates that allow you to insert your own pictures and wording. Also note, each picture has my social media handle so if these posts are shared, it always ties back to my brand.*

It's time to do some research again. Use the section below to list from most used to least used the social media platforms your customers will most likely engage with your beauty brand. Refer to Page 56 to see the demographics.

____

____

____

____

____

Why did you choose this platform (Hint: Refer to your ideal customer)?

____

____

____

____

____

**Tip – Each social media platform has an age range associated with its users. You will find mostly millennials (18-34) use Snapchat while Baby Boomers (51-69) are mostly on Facebook. Make sure you include in your research the age range of each listed on the previous page so you know which one may work best for your ideal customer.*

THE IMPORTANCE OF SOCIAL MEDIA NOTES

THE IMPORTANCE OF SOCIAL MEDIA NOTES

"Never start
a business
to 'make
money'.
Start a business
to make a
difference."
-Marie Forleo

7

HOW TO FUND YOUR BEAUTY BRAND

I'm sure you've gone through this workbook wondering when I would speak about how much it will cost to start your beauty brand. I promise you I didn't forget this very important aspect. Truth is, the reason I purposely saved this topic for last is because I didn't want you to be intimidated by cost or motivated by money. Instead I wanted you to see the value in what you have to offer and allow that to be your driving force. If I had mentioned money in the beginning you would've stopped right there. We often allow resources to kill our dreams before we even get started. Okay, I wont' prolong this any further, here are some costs you may incur to launch your beauty brand.

Description	Cost
Business License *(Incorporation Fee)*	$100 - $250
Insurance *(You want to cover yourself against customer issues such as claims of skin/scalp irritations, etc.)*	$500
Permits *(Resell, other permits dependent on state)*	$400
Products *(Handmade)*	$1,000 - $3,000
Products *(Mass produced)*	$2,000 - $4,000
Website	$300 - $500
Business Cards, other promotional items	$1,000
Storefront Start-Up Costs *(please see chapter 5 for more information on Store Fronts)*	$3,000 - $5,000
Professional Fees - *Accountant, Legal counsel, social media content expert, PR, brand strategist (Some of these costs are necessary immediately, others you may or may not need based on how fast you want to grow your brand)*	$2,000 - $3,000

**Tip – Keep in mind none of these costs are absolute and whenever possible, you should work to find ways to cut costs including bartering and collaborating.*

Keep in mind these costs are just estimates and it will take your research to determine what you need, what vendors you need, and how much product you think you need *(refer to Chapter 4).* In addition there will be a vast difference in start up costs for opening a storefront vs. online via your website or other online sites discussed in Chapter 6. But, this section is specifically to discuss how to fund your brand. Here are some suggestions but it's up to you to pin point where the money will come from.

•Grants/Loans
•Savings
•Investors (this can include family & friends)
•T-shirts, mugs, pens related to your business
•Go Fund Me

What other funding sources come to mind?

I know this is definitely the least fun part of creating your business and may even cause you to want to throw in the towel. But...DON'T GIVE UP! If everything you wanted to do was easy you may not appreciate the journey.

Here's another exercise for you, determine one of your products from *Chapter 3* (*Creating Your Products*) you think will be a huge hit by choosing the top 3 you know will be the top sellers. Release just one of these products and use it to fund the rest of your business. It will mean you have to go hard with that one product but it can be done.

____

____

____

____

____

____

You may not have all the financial resources you need right away but with hard work, you will get there.

HOW TO FUND YOUR BEAUTY BRAND NOTES

HOW TO FUND YOUR BEAUTY BRAND NOTES

YOU'VE GOT THIS

Thank you for allowing me to be a part of your journey as you work to create your own beauty brand. I sincerely hope this workbook gives you a foundation to what will be an exciting and fruitful time for you. Will you make mistakes along the way, absolutely but don't let them stop you. The saying goes that "Rome was not built in a day" and neither will your brand.

When I first began I honestly had no idea what I was doing and although there was some information out there, I found myself trying to piece it all together. It can be overwhelming to recreate the wheel so my hope is that this workbook will take some of the guess work out of it for you. But even as you work hard to make this happen, know that YOU'VE GOT THIS!

NOTES

NOTES

ADDITIONAL RESOURCES

Identifying Your Brand	
Kimberly Marie Clements *Branding Expert*	**www.hernameiskim.com**
Jasmine Powers *Marketing Expert*	**www.jasminepowers.com**

Creating Your Products	
Alibaba – *online resource to find mass produced vendors*	**www.alibaba.com**
Fiverr – *Low cost professionals to help with creating logos, marketing materials, and websites*	**www.fiverr.com**
U Printing – *Label Printing Service*	**www.uprinting.com**

Where to Sell Your Products	
Etsy - *Handmade Products*	**www.etsy.com**
Big Cartel – *ecommerce*	**www.bigcartel.com**
Square Space – *ecommerce*	**www.squarespace.com**
Shopify **-** *ecommerce*	**www.shopify.com**

ADDITIONAL RESOURCES

The Business of Beauty	
Small Business Administration - *Business Plan templates & other business related resources*	**www.sba.gov**
PayPal – *payment tool to accept credit cards*	**www.paypal.com**
Square - *payment tool to accept credit cards*	**www.squareup.com**

The Importance Of Social Media	
Facebook – *Join my online community to help with your journey*	**Unleash & Grow Your Own Beauty Brand (search)**
Canva – *helps with creating social media content and marketing materials*	**www.canva.com**

Useful Apps & Tools	
Pic Monkey – *picture editor*	**Available on iPhone & Android**
WordSwag – *generates cool text & fonts on your pictures*	**Available on iPhone & Android**
Rhonna Designs – *adds personality to your pictures with backgrounds and cool text*	**Available on iPhone & Android**
Mailchimp – *email integration marketing tool*	**www.mailchimp.com**

The first step is the hardest.
But it's totally worth it.
Moni B

www.ingramcontent.com/pod-product-compliance
Lightning Source LLC
Chambersburg PA
CBHW071229220526
45468CB00002B/773
* 9 7 8 1 9 7 4 5 0 0 1 7 8 *